Looking for Trouble

by the same author

FRIGHTENING TOYS (Faber)

US publications:

WALKING THE BLACK CAT
A WEDDING IN HELL
HOTEL INSOMNIA
THE BOOK OF GODS AND DEVILS
THE WORLD DOESN'T END
UNENDING BLUES
WEATHER FORECAST FOR UTOPIA AND VICINITY
SELECTED POEMS 1963–1983
AUSTERITIES
CLASSIC BALLROOM DANCES
CHARON'S COSMOLOGY
RETURN TO A PLACE LIT BY A GLASS OF MILK
DISMANTLING THE SILENCE

Looking for Trouble

CHARLES SIMIC

faber and faber
LONDON · BOSTON

First published in 1997
by Faber and Faber Limited
3 Queen Square London WC1N 3AU

Photoset by Wilmaset Ltd, Birkenhead, Wirral
Printed in England by Mackays of Chatham PLC, Chatham, Kent

© Charles Simic, 1997

Charles Simic is hereby identified as author of this
work in accordance with Section 77 of the Copyright,
Designs and Patents Act 1988

Poems from the following collections are reprinted by permission of
George Braziller, Inc.: *Dismantling the Silence*, copyright © 1971
by Charles Simic; *Return to a Place Lit by a Glass of Milk*,
copyright © 1974 by Charles Simic; *Charon's Cosmology*,
copyright © 1977 by Charles Simic; *Classic Ballroom Dances*,
copyright © 1980 by Charles Simic; *Austerities*,
copyright © 1982 by Charles Simic. Poems from
A Wedding in Hell and *Walking the Black Cat*
are reprinted by permission of Harcourt Brace & Company.

A CIP record for this book
is available from the British Library

ISBN 0-571-19233-5

2 4 6 8 10 9 7 5 3 1

Contents

Butcher Shop

Sometimes walking late at night
I stop before a closed butcher shop.
There is a single light in the store
Like the light in which the convict digs his tunnel.

An apron hangs on the hook:
The blood on it smeared into a map
Of the great continents of blood,
The great rivers and oceans of blood.

There are knives that glitter like altars
In a dark church
Where they bring the cripple and the imbecile
To be healed.

There is a wooden block where bones are broken,
Scraped clean – a river dried to its bed
Where I am fed,
Where deep in the night I hear a voice.

Tapestry

It hangs from heaven to earth.
There are trees in it, cities, rivers,
small pigs and moons. In one corner
the snow falling over a charging cavalry,
in another women are planting rice.

You can also see:
a chicken carried off by a fox,
a naked couple on their wedding night,
a column of smoke,
an evil-eyed woman spitting into a pail of milk.

What is behind it?
– Space, plenty of empty space.

And who is talking now?
– A man asleep under his hat.

What happens when he wakes up?
– He'll go into a barbershop.
They'll shave his beard, nose, ears and hair,
To make him look like everyone else.

Poem

Every morning I forget how it is.
I watch the smoke mount
In great strides above the city.
I belong to no one.

Then, I remember my shoes,
How I have to put them on,
How bending over to tie them up
I will look into the earth.

Bestiary for the Fingers
of My Right Hand

1

Thumb, loose tooth of a horse.
Rooster to his hens.
Horn of a devil. Fat worm
They have attached to my flesh
At the time of my birth.
It takes four to hold him down,
Bend him in half, until the bone
Begins to whimper.

Cut him off. He can take care
Of himself. Take root in the earth,
Or go hunting with wolves.

2

The second points the way.
True way. The path crosses the earth,
The moon and some stars.
Watch, he points further.
He points to himself.

3

The middle one has backache.
Stiff, still unaccustomed to this life;
An old man at birth. It's about something

That he had and lost,
That he looks for within my hand,
The way a dog looks
For fleas
With a sharp tooth.

4

The fourth is mystery.
Sometimes as my hand
Rests on the table
He jumps by himself
As though someone called his name.

After each bone, finger,
I come to him, troubled.

5

Something stirs in the fifth
Something perpetually at the point
Of birth. Weak and submissive,
His touch is gentle.
It weighs a tear.
It takes the mote out of the eye.

Fork

This strange thing must have crept
Right out of hell.
It resembles a bird's foot
Worn around the cannibal's neck.

As you hold it in your hand,
As you stab with it into a piece of meat,
It is possible to imagine the rest of the bird:
Its head which like your fist
Is large, bald, beakless and blind.

My Shoes

Shoes, secret face of my inner life:
Two gaping toothless mouths,
Two partly decomposed animal skins
Smelling of mice-nests.

My brother and sister who died at birth
Continuing their existence in you,
Guiding my life
Toward their incomprehensible innocence.

What use are books to me
When in you it is possible to read
The Gospel of my life on earth
And still beyond, of things to come?

I want to proclaim the religion
I have devised for your perfect humility
And the strange church I am building
With you as the altar.

Ascetic and maternal, you endure:
Kin to oxen, to Saints, to condemned men,
With your mute patience, forming
The only true likeness of myself.

Stone

Go inside a stone
That would be my way.
Let somebody else become a dove
Or gnash with a tiger's tooth.
I am happy to be a stone.

From the outside the stone is a riddle:
No one knows how to answer it.
Yet within, it must be cool and quiet
Even though a cow steps on it full weight,
Even though a child throws it in a river;
The stone sinks, slow, unperturbed
To the river bottom
Where the fishes come to knock on it
And listen.

I have seen sparks fly out
When two stones are rubbed,
So perhaps it is not dark inside after all;
Perhaps there is a moon shining
From somewhere, as though behind a hill –
Just enough light to make out
The strange writings, the star-charts
On the inner walls.

Brooms

for Tomaz, Susan and George

1

Only brooms
Know the devil
Still exists,

That the snow grows whiter
After a crow has flown over it,
That a dark dusty corner
Is the place of dreamers and children,

That a broom is also a tree
In the orchard of the poor,
That a hanging roach there
Is a mute dove.

2

Brooms appear in dreambooks
As omens of approaching death.
This is their secret life.
In public, they act like flat-chested old maids
Preaching temperance.

They are sworn enemies of lyric poetry.
In prison they accompany the jailer,
Enter cells to hear confessions.

Their short-end comes down
When you least expect it.

Left alone behind a door
Of a condemned tenement,
They mutter to no one in particular,
Words like *virgin wind moon-eclipse*,
And that most sacred of all names:
Hieronymous Bosch.

3

In this and in no other manner
Was the first ancestral broom made:
Namely, they plucked all the arrows
From the bent back of Saint Sebastian.
They tied them with a rope
On which Judas hung himself.
Stuck in the stilt
On which Copernicus
Touched the morning star.

Then the broom was ready
To leave the monastery.
The dust welcomed it –
That great pornographer
Immediately wanted to
Look under its skirt.

4

The secret teaching of brooms
Excludes optimism, the consolation

Of laziness, the astonishing wonders
Of a glass of aged moonshine.

It says: the bones end up under the table.
Bread-crumbs have a mind of their own.
The milk is you-know-who's semen.
The mice have the last squeal.

As for the famous business
Of levitation, I suggest remembering:
There is only one God
And his prophet is Mohammed.

5

And then finally there's your grandmother
Sweeping the dust of the nineteenth century
Into the twentieth, and your grandfather plucking
A straw out of the broom to pick his teeth.

Long winter nights.
Dawns a thousand years deep.
Kitchen windows like heads
Bandaged for toothache.

The broom beyond them sweeping,
Tucking in the lucent grains of dust
Into neat pyramids,
That have tombs in them,

Already sacked by robbers,
Once, long ago.

Watermelons

Green Buddhas
On the fruit stand.
We eat the smile
And spit out the teeth.

Traveling

I turn myself into a sack.
An old ragpicker
Takes me out at dawn.
We go shuffling, we go stooped.

Here he says is the blue tie,
A man climbed it as it hung from his neck.
He's up there sobbing now
For he doesn't know how to come down.

But I say nothing, what can a sack say?

Here he says is the overcoat.
His name is Ahab, his tatters are our tatters.
He is searching for the tailor who made him.
He wants all his black threads ripped out.

But I say nothing, what can a sack say?

Here he says are the boots,
As they sunk, as they went under
They saw their lives in a flash,
They'll cling to us wherever we go.

But I say nothing, what can a sack
Stuffed to its throat say?

The Place

They were talking about the war,
The table still uncleared in front of them.
Across the way, the first window
Of the evening was already lit.
He sat, hunched over, quiet,
The old fear coming over him . . .
It grew darker. She got up to take the plate –
Now unpleasantly white – to the kitchen.
Outside in the fields, in the woods
A bird spoke in proverbs,
A Pope went out to meet Attila,
The ditch was ready for its squad.

Solitude

There now, where the first crumb
Falls from the table
You think no one hears it
As it hits the floor

But somewhere already
The ants are putting on
Their Quakers' hats
And setting out to visit you.

The Chicken without a Head

When two times two was three,
The chicken without a head was hatched.
When the earth was still flat,
It fell off its edge, daydreaming.
When there were 13 signs in the zodiac,
It found a dead star for its gizzard.
When the first fox was getting married,
It taught itself to fly with one wing.
When all the eggs were still golden,
The clouds in the sky tasted like sweet corn.
When the rain flooded its coop,
Its wishbone was its arc.
Ah, when the chicken had only itself to roast,
The lightning was its skewer,
The thunder its baste and salt.

The chicken without a head made a sigh,
And then a hailstone out of that sigh,
And the window for the hailstone to strike.
Nine lives it made for itself,
And nine coats of solitude to dress them in.
It made its own shadow. No, I'm lying.
It only made a flea to bite some holes in the shadow.
Made it all out of nothing. Made a needle
To sew back its broken eggshell.

Made the lovers naked. Everybody else put clothes on them.
Its father made the knife, but it polished the blade,
Until it threw back its image like a funhouse mirror.
Made it all out of raglets of time.
Who's to say it'd be happier if it didn't?

3

Hear the song of a chicken without a head
As it goes scratching in grave-dirt.
A song in which two parallel lines
Meet at infinity, in which God
Makes the last of the little apples,
In which golden fleece is heard growing
On a sad girl's pubis. The song
Of swearwords dreaming of a pure mouth.
The song of a doornail raised from the dead.
The song of circumspection because accomplices
Have been found, because the egg's safe
In the cuckoo's nest. The song
You wade into until your own hat floats.
A song of contagious laughter.
A lethal song.
That's right, the song of premonition.

4

On a headless evening of a headless day
The chicken on fire and the words
Around it like a ring of fabulous beasts.
Each night it threw them a bite-sized portion of its heart.
The words were hungry, the night held the fork.
Whatever our stylish gallows-bird made, its head unmade,

Its long lost, axed-off sultan's head
Rose into the sky in a balloon of fiery numerals.
Down below the great feast went on:
The table that supplies itself with bread.
A saw that cuts a dream in half.
Wings so quick they don't get wet in heavy rain.
The egg that mutters to the frying pan:
I swear it by the hair in my yolk,
There's no such thing as a chicken without a head.

5

The chicken without a head ran a maze,
Ran half-plucked,
A serving fork stuck in its back,
Ran, backwards, into the blue of the evening.
Ran upsidedown,
Its drumsticks and talons in the clouds.
Someone huge and red-aproned rose in its wake.
Many black umbrellas parting to let it pass.
Ran leaving its squinting head far behind,
Its head reeking of barber's cologne.
Ran up the church steeple,
Up the lightning rod on that steeple
For the wind to hone its prettiest plumes.
Ran, and is still running this Good Friday,
Between raindrops,
Hellfoxes on its trail.

White

What is that little black thing I see there in the white?

Walt Whitman

I

Out of poverty
To begin again

With the taste of silence
On my tongue

Say a word,
Then listen to it fray

Thread by thread,
In the fading,

The already vanishing
Evening light.

*

So clear, it's obscure
The sense of existing

In this very moment,
Cheek by jowl with

My shadow on the wall,
Watching and listening,

[19]

With its gallows-like
Contorted neck

Bloodied by the sunset,
To my own heart beat.

                    *

This is breath, only breath.
Think it over, friend.

A shit-house fly weighs
Twice as much.

But when I tell the world so,
I'm less by a breath.

The struck match flares up
And nods in agreement

Before the dark claps it
With its heavy hands.

                    *

As strange as a shepherd
In the Arctic Circle.

Someone like Bo-peep.
All her sheep are white

And she can't get any sleep
Over lost sheep,

And she's got a flute
Which cries Bo-peep,

Which says, poor girl,
Take care of your sheep.

*

On a late afternoon of snow,
In a small unlit grocery store

Where a door has just opened
With a long, painful squeak,

A small boy carries a piece of paper
Between his thumb and forefinger

For the squint-eyed old woman
Bending low over the counter.

It's that paper I'm remembering,
And the quiet and the shadows.

*

You're not what you seem to be.
I'm not what I seem to be.

It's as if we were the unknowing
Inmates of someone's shadowbox,

And the curtain was our breath
And so were the stage sets

Which were like the world we know,
His gloves gray as the sky

While he holds us up by our feet
Swaying over the earth to and fro.

*

We need a marrying preacher.
Some crow, praise be,

By the side of the road
With a sun-reddened beak

Studying a wind-leafed
Black book

All of whose pages are gold-edged
And blank,

As we wait, with frost thickening
On our eyelashes.

*

The sky of the desert,
The heavens of the crucified.

The great white sky
Of the visionaries.

Its one lone, ghost-like
Buzzard hovering,

Writing the long century's
Obituary column

Over the white city,
The city of our white nights.

*

Mother gives me to the morning
On the threshold.

I have the steam of my breath
As my bride.

The snow on my shoes
Is the hems of her wedding dress,

My love always a step ahead,
Always a blur,

A white-out
In the raging, dream-like storm.

*

As if I shut my eyes
In order to peek

At the world unobserved,
And saw

The nameless
In its glory.

And knew no way
To speak of it,

And did, nevertheless,
And then said something else.

2

What are you up to smartass?
I turn on my tongue's skewer.

What do you baste yourself with?
I spit bile laced with blood.

Do you sprinkle pepper and salt?
I bite words as they come into my mouth.

And how will you know you're done?
My eyes will burn till I see clear.

What will you carve yourself with?
I'll let my tongue be the knife.

*

In the inky forest,
In its maziest,

Murkiest scribble
Of words

And wordless cries,
I went for a glimpse

Of the blossom-like
White erasure

Over a huge,
Furiously crossed-out something.

*

I can't say I'm much of a cook,
If my heart is in the fire with the onions.

I can't say I'm much of a hero,
If the weight of my head has me pinned down.

I can't say I'm the boss here,
If the flies hang their hats in my mouth.

I can't say I got the smarts,
If I expect the stars in the sky to answer me.

Nor can I call myself good-for-nothing.
Thanks to me the worms will have their feast.

*

One has to make do.
Make ends meet,

Odds and ends.
Make no bones about it.

Make a stab in the dark.
Make the hair curl.

Make a door-to-nowhere.
Make a megaphone with my hands,

And call and make do
With the silence answering.

*

Then all's well and white
Even at midnight.

The highways are snowbound,
The forest paths are hushed.

The power lines have fallen.
The windows are dark.

Nothing but starlight
And snow's dim light

And the wind wildly
Preaching in the pines.

*

In an unknown year
Of an all-evil century,

On a day of frost and biting wind,
A tiny old woman,

One foot in the grave,
Met a boy playing hooky.

She offered him a sugar cube
In a hand so wizened

His tongue twisted into a noose
Saying thanks.

*

Do you take this line
Stretching to infinity?

I take this white paper
Lying still before me.

Do you take this ring
That has no known circumference?

I take this breath
Slipping in and out of it.

Then you may kiss the dot
Where your pencil fell on its lead.

*

Had to get through me
On its long trek

To and from nowhere.
Woe to every heartbeat

That stood in its way,
Woe to every thought . . .

Time's white ants,
The rustle of their feet.

Gravedigger ants.
Village-idiot ants.

*

I haven't ventured far.
Five fingers crumpled up

Over the blank page
Like a love letter,

Do you hear the white night
Touching down?

I hear the ear-trumpets,
The holy escutcheons

Turning golden
In the dying light.

*

Psst. The white hair
Fallen from my head

On the writing paper
Momentarily unidentified.

I had to bend down low
And put my eye next to it

To make sure,
Then nudge it, ever-so-slowly

With the long tip of my pen
Over the edge of the table.

What the White Had to Say

Because I'm nothing you can name,
I knew you long before you knew me.
Some days you keep your hand closed
As if you've caught me,
But it's just a fly you've got there.
No use calling on angels and devils
In the middle of the night.
First thing in the morning, squint
Into the dregs of your coffee cup for all I care.
I do not answer to your hocus-pocus,
For I'm closer to you than your breath.
One sun shines on us both
Through a crack in your eyelids.
Your open hand shows me off
To the four white walls,
While with my tail I wave the fly away,
But there's no tail and the fly
Is a thought buzzing in your head.

Because I'm nothing you'll ever name
You twist your tongue hoping to skewer me.
The ear that rose at four in the morning
Desiring to hear the truth inside a word.

Listen to this, my dear nothing,
I'm the great nothing that tucks you to sleep,
The finger placed softly on your lips
That makes you sit up in bed wide awake.
Still, the riddle comes with no answer.
The same unknown mother left us on a doorstep,
The same four walls made us insomniac.
Late-night piano picking out blue notes,
I'm that intangible something between them,
And still you want me to say more,
And so we can never get past the beginning.
Time has stopped. Your shadow
With its gallows-like crooked neck
Has not stirred on the wall.

The Partial Explanation

Seems like a long time
Since the waiter took my order.
Grimy little luncheonette,
The snow falling outside.

Seems like it has grown darker
Since I last heard the kitchen door
Behind my back,
Since I last noticed
Anyone pass on the street.

A glass of ice water
Keeps me company
At this table I chose myself
Upon entering.

And a longing,
Incredible longing
To eavesdrop
On the conversation
Of cooks.

A Landscape with Crutches

So many crutches. Now even the daylight
Needs one, even the smoke
As it goes up. And the shacks –
One per customer – they move off
In a single file with difficulty,

I said, with a hell of an effort . . .
And the trees behind them about to stumble,
And the ants on their toy-crutches,
And the wind on its ghost-crutch.

I can't get any peace around here:
The bread on its artificial limbs,
A headless doll in a wheelchair,
And my mother, mind you, using
Two knives for crutches as she squats to pee.

Nursery Rhyme

The little pig goes to market.
Historical necessity. I like to recite
While you prefer to write on the blackboard.
Leap frog and marbles.

Their heads are big and their noses are short.
Lovely afternoon. The firing squad.
A street maimed so it can go on begging.
Eternal recurrence and its trash heap.

Follow your calling, we follow ours.
The soldier's hand is gentle. The green meadow.
People who snore have happy dreams.
Our father in heaven loves us all.

A pig with gold teeth, says the barber.
Banks of a river lined with willows.
Now someone's kicking him to hurry up.
Rope, give a drink of milk to the rope.

I need another cigarette quickly.
An execution. The old wedding photograph.
I see a blur, a speck, meager, receding,
Our lives trailing in its wake.

Help Wanted

They ask for a knife
I come running
They need a lamb
I introduce myself as the lamb

A thousand sincere apologies
It seems they require some rat-poison
They require a shepherd
For their flock of black widows

Luckily I've brought my bloody
Letters of recommendation
I've brought my death certificate
Signed and notarized

But they've changed their minds again
Now they want a song-bird a bit of springtime
They want a woman
To soap and kiss their balls

It's one of my many talents
(I assure them)
Chirping and whistling like an aviary
Spreading the cheeks of my ass

Animal Acts

A bear who eats with a silver spoon.
Two apes adept at grave-digging.
Rats who do calculus.
A police dog who copulates with a woman,
Who takes undertaker's measurements.

A bedbug who suffers, who has doubts
About his existence. The miraculous
Laughing dove. A thousand-year-old turtle
Playing billiards. A chicken who
Cuts his own throat, who bleeds.

The trainer with his sugar-cubes,
With his chair and whip. The evenings
When they all huddle in a cage,
Smoking cheap cigars, lazily
Marking the cards in the new deck.

A Wall

That's the only image
That turns up.

A wall all by itself,
Poorly lit, beckoning,
But no sense of the room,
Not even a hint
Of why it is I remember
So little and so clearly:

The fly I was watching,
The details of its wings
Glowing like turquoise.
Its feet, to my amusement
Following a minute crack –
An eternity
Around that simple event.

And nothing else; and nowhere
To go back to;
And no one else
As far as I know to verify.

Eyes Fastened with Pins

How much death works,
No one knows what a long
Day he puts in. The little
Wife always alone
Ironing death's laundry.
The beautiful daughters
Setting death's supper table.
The neighbors playing
Pinochle in the backyard
Or just sitting on the steps
Drinking beer. Death,
Meanwhile, in a strange
Part of town looking for
Someone with a bad cough,
But the address somehow wrong,
Even death can't figure it out
Among all the locked doors . . .
And the rain beginning to fall.
Long windy night ahead.
Death with not even a newspaper
To cover his head, not even
A dime to call the one pining away,
Undressing slowly, sleepily,
And stretching naked
On death's side of the bed.

Prodigy

I grew up bent over
a chessboard.

I loved the word *endgame*.

All my cousins looked worried.

It was a small house
near a Roman graveyard.
Planes and tanks
shook its windowpanes.

A retired professor of astronomy
taught me how to play.

That must have been in 1944.

In the set we were using,
the paint had almost chipped off
the black pieces.

The white King was missing
and had to be substituted for.

I'm told but do not believe
that that summer I witnessed
men hung from telephone poles.

I remember my mother
blindfolding me a lot.

She had a way of tucking my head
suddenly under her overcoat.

In chess, too, the professor told me,
the masters play blindfolded,
the great ones on several boards
at the same time.

Baby Pictures of Famous Dictators

The epoch of a streetcar drawn by horses;
The organ-grinder and his monkey.
Women with parasols. Little kids in rowboats
Photographed against a cardboard backdrop depicting
    an idyllic sunset
At the fairgrounds where they all went to see
The two-headed calf, the bearded
Fat lady who dances the dance of seven veils.

And the great famine raging through India . . .
Fortune-telling white rats pulling a card out of shoebox
While Edison worries over the lightbulb,
And the first model of the sewing machine
Is delivered in a pushcart
To a modest white-fenced home in the suburbs,

Where there are always a couple of infants
Posing for the camera in their sailors' suits,
Out there in the garden overgrown with shrubs.
Lovable little mugs smiling faintly toward
The new century. Innocent. Why not?
All of them like ragdolls of the period
With those chubby porcelain heads
That shut their long eyelashes as you lay them down.

In a kind of perpetual summer twilight . . .
One can even make out the shadow of the tripod and
    the black hood

That must have been quivering in the breeze.
One assumes that they all stayed up late squinting at the
   stars,
And were carried off to bed by their mothers and big
   sisters,
While the dogs remained behind:
Pedigreed bitches pregnant with bloodhounds.

Shirt

To get into it
As it lies
Crumpled on the floor
Without disturbing a single crease

Respectful
Of the way I threw it down
Last night
The way it happened to land

Almost managing
The impossible contortions
Doubling back now
Through a knotted sleeve

The Stream

for Russ Banks

The ear threading
the eye

all night long
the ear
on a long errand
for the eye

through the thickening
pine
white birch
over no man's land

pebbles
is it
compact in their anonymity
their gravity

accidents of location
abstract necessity

water
which takes such pains
to convince me
it is flowing

*

Summoning me
to be
two places at once

to drift
the length
of its chill
its ache

hand white
at the knuckles

live bait
the old hide and seek
in and out
of the swirl

luminous verb
carnivorous verb
innocent as sand
under its blows

*

An insomnia as big
as the stars'

always
on the brink –
as it were
of some deeper utterance

[44]

some harsher
reckoning

at daybreak

lightly
oh so lightly
when she brushes
against me

and the hems of her long skirt
go trailing

a bit longer

*

Nothing
that comes to nothing
for company

comes the way a hurt
the way a thought
comes

comes and keeps coming

all night meditating
on what she asks of me
when she doesn't

when I hear myself say
she doesn't

[45]

Harsh Climate

The brain itself in its skull
Is very cold,
According to
Albertus Magnus.

Something like a stretch of tundra
On the scale of the universe.
Galactic wind.
Lofty icebergs in the distance.

Polar night.
A large ocean liner caught in the ice.
A few lights still burning on the deck.
Silence and fierce cold.

Window Washer

And again the screech of the scaffold
High up there where all our thoughts converge:
Lightheaded, hung
By a leather strap,

Twenty stories up
In the chill of late November
Wiping the grime
Off the pane, the many windows

Which have no way of opening,
Tinted windows mirroring the clouds
That are like equestrian statues,
Phantom liberators with sabers raised

Before these dark offices,
And their anonymous multitudes
Bent over this day's
Wondrously useless labor.

In Midsummer Quiet

Ariadne's bird,
That lone
Whip-poor-will.

Ball of twilight-thread
Unraveling furtively.
Tawny thread,
Raw, pink the thread-end.

A claw or two also
To pare, snip . . .
After which it sits still
For the stream to explain why it shivers

So.
  Resuming, farther on,
Intermittently,
By the barn
Where the first stars are –
In quotation marks,
As it were – O phantom

Bird!
Dreaming of my own puzzles
And mazes.

Strictly Bucolic

for Mark and Jules

Are these mellifluous sheep,
And these the meadows made twice-melliferous by their
    bleating?
Is that the famous mechanical wind-up shepherd
Who comes with instructions and service manual?

This must be the regulation white fleece
Bleached and starched to perfection,
And we could be posing for our first communion pictures,
Except for the nasty horns.

I am beginning to think this might be
The Angelic Breeders Association's
Millennial Company Picnic (all expenses paid)
With a few large black dogs as special guests.

These dogs serve as ushers and usherettes.
They're always studying the rules,
The exigencies of proper deportment,
When they're not reading Theocritus,

Or wagging their tails at the approach of
Theodora. Or is it Theodosius? Or even Theodoric?
They're theomorfic, of course. They theologize.
Theogony is their favorite. They also love theomachy.

Now they hand out the blue ribbons.
Ah, there's one for everyone!
Plus the cauldrons of stinking cabbage and boiled turnips
Which don't figure in this idyll.

Austerities

From the heel
Of a half loaf
Of black bread,
They made a child's head.

Child, they said,
We've nothing for eyes,
Nothing to spare for ears
And nose.

Just a knife
To make a slit
Where your mouth
Ought to be.

You can grin,
You can eat,
Spit the crumbs
Into our faces.

Thus

Blue devils'
Bluest
Offspring –
My wife.

I said,
Pascal's own
Prize abyssologist
In marriage.

On her knees
Still scrubbing
The marble stairs
Of a Russian countess.

Once long ago in Paris
Gathering the butts
Outside the fashionable cafés
For her unemployed father.

Or in the New World
Naked before the grim
Doctor and nurse
A murmur in the heart.

Nevertheless, poking
The spit-moistened

End of a black thread
At the unblinking needle's eye,

Twelve hours a day.
A sublime seamstress,
An occupation hard on the backbone
And the eyesight.

On dark winter Sundays
Difficult to squint out
The letters and foreign words
In the night school textbook.

All the carefully dog-eared,
Underlined passages
About lynchings, tar-featherings,
Witch-burnings –

Next to a cup of black coffee –
The kind storefront gypsies make
When they sit staring at the rain,
Their lips just barely moving.

My Weariness of Epic Proportions

I like it when
Achilles
Gets killed
And even his buddy Patroclus –
And that hothead Hector –
And the whole Greek and Trojan
Jeunesse dorée
Is more or less
Expertly slaughtered
So there's finally
Peace and quiet
(The gods having momentarily
Shut up)
One can hear
A bird sing
And a daughter ask her mother
Whether she can go to the well
And of course she can
By that lovely little path
That winds through
The olive orchard

Madonnas Touched Up with a Goatee

Most ancient Metaphysics, (poor Metaphysics!)
All decked up in imitation jewelry.
We went for a stroll, arm in arm, smooching in public
Despite the difference in ages.

It's still the 19th century, she whispered.
We were in a knife-fighting neighborhood
Among some rundown relics of the Industrial Revolution.
Just a little further, she assured me,
In the back of a certain candy store only she knew about,
The customers were engrossed in the *Phenomenology of
    the Spirit*.

It's long past midnight, my dove, my angel!
We'd better be careful, I thought.
There were young hoods on street corners
With crosses and iron studs on their leather jackets.
They all looked like they'd read Darwin and that madman
    Pavlov,
And were about to ask us for a light.

The Great Horned Owl

One morning the Grand Seigneur
Is so good as to appear.
He sits in a scrawny little tree
In my backyard.

When I say his name aloud,
He turns his head
And looks at me
In utter disbelief.

I show him my belt,
How I had to
Tighten it lately
To the final hole.

He ruffles his feathers,
Studies the empty woodshed,
The old red Chevy on blocks.
Alas! He's got to be going.

Midpoint

No sooner had I left A.
Than I started doubting its existence:
Its streets and noisy crowds;
Its famous all-night cafés and prisons.

It was dinnertime. The bakeries were closing:
Their shelves empty and white with flour.
The grocers were lowering their iron-grilles.
A lovely young woman was buying the last casaba
    melon.

Even the back alley where I was born
Blurs, dims . . . O rooftops!
Armadas of bedsheets and shirts
In the blustery, crimson dusk . . .

*

B. at which I am destined
To arrive by and by
Doesn't exist now. Hurriedly
They're building it for my arrival,

And on that day it will be ready:
Its streets and noisy crowds . . .
Even the schoolhouse where I first
Forged my father's signature . . .

Knowing that on the day
Of my departure
It will vanish forever
Just as A. did.

Miracle Glass Co.

Heavy mirror carried
Across the street,
I bow to you
And to everything that appears in you,
Momentarily
And never again the same way:

This street with its pink sky,
Row of gray tenements,
A lone dog,
Children on rollerskates,
Woman buying flowers,
Someone looking lost.

In you, mirror framed in gold
And carried across the street
By someone I can't even see,
To whom, too, I bow.

Late Arrival

The world was already here,
Serene in its otherness.
It only took you to arrive
On the late afternoon train
To where no one awaited you.

A town no one ever remembered
Because of its drabness,
Where you lost your way
Searching for a place to stay
In a maze of identical streets.

It was then that you heard,
As if for the very first time,
The sound of your own footsteps
Under a church clock
Which had stopped just as you did

Between two empty streets
Aglow in the afternoon sunlight,
Two modest stretches of infinity
For you to wonder at
Before resuming your walk.

Tattooed City

I, who am only an incomprehensible
Bit of scribble
On some warehouse wall
Or some subway entrance.

Matchstick figure,
Heart pierced by arrow,
Scratch of a meter maid
On a parked hearse.

CRAZY CHARLIE in red spraypaint
Crowding for warmth
With other unknown divinities
In an underpass at night.

Dream Avenue

Monumental, millennial decrepitude,
As tragedy requires. A broad
Avenue with trash unswept,
A few solitary speck-sized figures
Going about their business
In a world already smudged by a schoolboy's eraser.

You've no idea what city this is,
What country? It could be a dream,
But is it yours? You're nothing
But a vague sense of loss,
A piercing, heart-wrenching dread
On an avenue with no name

With a few figures conveniently small
And blurred who, in any case,
Have their backs to you
As they look elsewhere, beyond
The long row of gray buildings and their many windows,
Some of which appear broken.

The Dead in Photographs

They were all mere beginners.
They stood still for the camera,
Only a few thinking to move
And make a blur at the right moment.

Others held their smiles seemingly forever.
It was their wedding day.
Here they were by the side of the road
On the way to California.
The groom had a wide tie on with green parrots.
The bride wore a straw hat
With a topping of strawberries.

In Los Angeles it was Sunday morning.
The photographer took a picture
Of a closed barber shop,
A black cat crossing an empty avenue,
A tall palm tree in the wind.

Then the dead reappeared.
A blind man stood on a street corner
Playing the guitar and singing.
The little boy walked up to the camera
And stuck out his tongue at us.

Madame Thebes

That awful deceit of appearances.
Some days
Everything looks unfamiliar
On my street.
It's somebody else's life I'm living.

An immaculate silent order
Of white buildings and dark clouds,
And then the open door
In a house with lowered voices.
Someone left in a hurry,
And they're waiting for me to come in
With a lit match.

There's a rustle of a long skirt,
But when I enter
It's only the evening papers
Sliding off the table
Bird-like
In a large and drafty
And now altogether empty room.

The Clocks of the Dead

One night I went to keep the clock company.
It had a loud tick after midnight
As if it were uncommonly afraid.
It's like whistling past a graveyard,
I explained.
In any case, I told him I understood.

Once there were clocks like that
In every kitchen in America.
Now the factory's windows are all broken.
The old men on night shift are in Charon's boat.
The day you stop, I said to the clock,
The little wheels they keep in reserve
Will have rolled away
Into many hard-to-find places.

Just thinking about it, I forgot to wind the clock.
We woke up in the dark.
How quiet the city is, I said.
Like the clocks of the dead, my wife replied.
Grandmother on the wall,
I heard the snows of your childhood
Begin to fall.

This Morning

Enter without knocking, hard-working ant.
I'm just sitting here mulling over
What to do this dark, overcast day.
It was a night of the radio turned low,
Fitful sleep, vague, troubling dreams.
I woke up lovesick and confused.
I thought I heard Estella in the garden singing
And some bird answering her,
But it was the rain. Dark treetops swaying
And whispering. 'Come to me, my desire,'
I said. And she came to me by and by,
Her breath smelling of mint, her tongue
Wetting my cheek, and then she vanished.
Slowly day came, a gray streak of daylight
To bathe my hands and face in.
Hours passed, and then you crawled
Under the door, and stopped before me.
You visit the same tailors the mourners do,
Mr Ant. I like the silence between us,
The quiet – that holy state even the rain
Knows about. Listen to her begin to fall,
As if with eyes closed,
Muting each drop in her wild-beating heart.

Pocket Theater

Fingers in an overcoat pocket. Fingers sticking out of a black leather glove. The nails chewed raw. One play is called 'Thieves' Market', another 'Night in a Dime Museum'. The fingers when they strip are like bewitching nude bathers or the fake wooden limbs in a cripple factory. No one ever sees the play: you put your hand in somebody else's pocket on the street and feel the action.

Crazy about Her Shrimp

We don't even take time
To come up for air.
We keep our mouths full and busy
Eating bread and cheese
And smooching in between.

No sooner have we made love
Than we are back in the kitchen.
While I chop the hot peppers,
She wiggles her ass
And stirs the shrimp on the stove.

How good the wine tastes
That has run red
Out of a laughing mouth!
Down her chin
And onto her naked tits.

'I'm getting fat,' she says,
Turning this way and that way
Before the mirror.
'I'm crazy about her shrimp!'
I shout to the gods above.

Transport

In the frying pan
On the stove
I found my love
And me naked.

Chopped onions
Fell on our heads
And made us cry.
It's like a parade,
I told her, confetti
When some guy
Reaches the moon.

'Means of transport,'
She replied obscurely
While we fried.
'Means of transport!'

Love Flea

He took a flea
From her armpit
To keep

And cherish
In a matchbox,
Even pricking his finger

From time to time
To feed it
Drops of blood.

What I Overheard

In summer's idle time,
When trees grow heavy with leaves
And spread shade everywhere
That is a delight to lie in
Alone
Or in the company of a dear friend,

Dreaming or having a quiet talk
Without looking at each other,
Until she feels drowsy
As if after too much wine,
And you draw close for a kiss
On her cheek, and instead
Stay with lips pursed, listening

To a bee make its rounds lazily,
And a far-off rooster crow
On the edge of sleep with the leaves hushed
Or rustling, ever so softly,
About something or other on their mind.

Where the Dreamy Wabash Flows

A world's disappearing.
Little street,
You were too narrow,
Too much in the shade already.

You had only one dog,
One lone child.
You hid your biggest mirror,
Your undressed lovers.

Someone carted them off
In an open truck.
They were still embraced traveling
On their sofa

Over a darkening plain,
Some unknown Kansas or Nebraska
With a storm brewing.
The woman opening a red umbrella

In the truck. The boy
And the dog running after them,
As if after a rooster
With its head chopped off.

Reading History

for Hans Magnus

At times, reading here
In the library,
I'm given a glimpse
Of those condemned to death
Centuries ago,
And of their executioners.
I see each pale face before me
The way a judge
Pronouncing a sentence would,
Marveling at the thought
That I do not exist yet.

With eyes closed I can hear
The evening birds.
Soon they will be quiet
And the final night on earth
Will commence
In the fullness of its sorrow.

How vast, dark, and impenetrable
Are the early morning skies
Of those led to their death
In a world from which I'm entirely absent,
Where I can still watch
Someone's slumped back,

Someone who is walking away from me
With his hands tied,
His graying head still on his shoulders,
Someone who
In what little remains of his life
Knows in some vague way about me,
And thinks of me as God,
As Devil.

Psalm

You've been a long time making up your mind,
O Lord, about these madmen
Running the world. Their reach is long
And their claws must have frightened you.

One of them found me with his shadow.
The day turned chill. I dangled
Between terror and valor
In the darkest corner of my son's bedroom.

I sought with my eyes, You in whom I do not believe.
You've been busy making the flowers pretty,
The lambs run after their mother,
Or perhaps you haven't been doing even that?

It was spring. The killers were full of sport
And merriment, and your divines
Were right at their side, to make sure
Our final goodbyes were said properly.

Empires

My grandmother prophesied the end
Of your empires, O fools!
She was ironing. The radio was on.
The earth trembled beneath our feet.

One of your heroes was giving a speech.
'Monster,' she called him.
There were cheers and gun salutes for the monster.
'I could kill him with my bare hands,'
She announced to me.

There was no need to. They were all
Going to the devil any day now.
'Don't go blabbering about this to anyone,'
She warned me.
And pulled my ear to make sure I understood.

The Story of the Crucifixion

In which the roles are played
By our dearest friends.
Their children are the beggars.
Their purebred dogs the Roman soldiers.

They are climbing a bare hill
On a windy day in spring.
The clouds are rushing ahead of them
As if to be there first.

A number of solitary figures
Stand apart waving their arms.
They all want the part
Of the long-suffering Saviour for themselves.

Windy day. A bare hill
Like the closely cropped head of a convict.
The dogs like Roman soldiers,
The children like swarming beggars.

Romantic Landscape

To grieve, always to suffer
At the thought of time passing.
The outside world shadowy
As your deepest self.
Melancholy meadows, trees so still,
They seem afraid of themselves.

The sunset sky for one brief moment
Radiant with some supreme insight,
And then it's over. Tragic theater:
Blood and mourning at which
Even the birds fall silent.

Spirit, you who are everywhere and nowhere,
Watch over the lost lamb
Now that the mouth of the Infinite
Opens over us
And its dumb tongue begins to move darkly.

Prayer

You who know only the present moment,
O Lord,
You who remember nothing
Of what came before,
Who admire the beauty
Of a dead child,
The lovers embraced
In a field of yellow flowers.

The game of chess
And the cracks on the poorhouse wall
Are equally interesting
And incomprehensible to You
Who know what it's like to be a tiger,
A mouse in the instant of danger,
And know nothing of my regrets,
My solitudes,
And my infinite horror of You.

Imported Novelties

They didn't answer to repeated knocks,
Or perhaps they were in no hurry.
On the eighteenth floor
Even the sunlight moved lazily
Past the floating dust.
A year could pass here, I thought,
As in a desert solitude.

'Unknown parties, rarely seen,'
The elevator operator warned me.
He wore a New Year's party hat in August;
I was looking for work.

Inside, I imagined rows of file cabinets,
Old desks, dead telephones.
I could have been sitting at one of them myself,
Like someone doused with gasoline
In the moment before the match is lit,

But then the elevator took me down.

Via del Tritone

In Rome, on the street of that name,
I was walking alone in the sun
In the noonday heat, when I saw a house
With shutters closed, the sight of which
Pained me so much, I could have
Been born there and left inconsolably.

The ochre walls, the battered old door
I was tempted to push open and didn't,
Knowing already the coolness of the entrance,
The garden with a palm tree beyond,
And the dark stairs on the left.

Shutters closed to cool shadowy rooms
With impossibly high ceilings,
And here and there a watery mirror
And my pale and contorted face
To greet me and startle me again and again.

'You found what you were looking for,'
I expected someone to whisper.
But there was no one, neither there
Nor in the street, which was deserted
In that monstrous heat that gives birth
To false memories and tritons.

Mirrors at 4 a.m.

You must come to them sideways
In rooms webbed in shadow,
Sneak a view of their emptiness
Without them catching
A glimpse of you in return.

The secret is,
Even the empty bed is a burden to them,
A pretense.
They are more themselves keeping
The company of a blank wall,
The company of time and eternity

Which, begging your pardon,
Cast no image
As they admire themselves in the mirror,
While you stand to the side
Pulling a hanky out
To wipe your brow surreptitiously.

Emily's Theme

My dear trees, I no longer recognize you
In that wintry light.
You brought me a reminder I can do without:
The world is old, it was always old,
There's nothing new in it this afternoon.
The garden could've been a padlocked window
Of a pawnshop I was studying
With every item in it dust-covered.

Each one of my thoughts was being ghostwritten
By anonymous authors. Each time they hit
A cobwebbed typewriter key, I shudder.
Luckily, dark came quickly today.
Soon the neighbors were burning leaves,
And perhaps a few other things too.
Later, I saw the children run around the fire,
Their faces demonic in its flames.

Cameo Appearance

I had a small, nonspeaking part
In a bloody epic. I was one of the
Bombed and fleeing humanity.
In the distance our great leader
Crowed like a rooster from a balcony,
Or was it a great actor
Impersonating our great leader?

That's me there, I said to the kiddies.
I'm squeezed between the man
With two bandaged hands raised
And the old woman with her mouth open
As if she were showing us a tooth

That hurts badly. The hundred times
I rewound the tape, not once
Could they catch sight of me
In that huge gray crowd,
That was like any other gray crowd.

Trot off to bed, I said finally.
I know I was there. One take
Is all they had time for.
We ran, and the planes grazed our hair,
And then they were no more
As we stood dazed in the burning city,
But, of course, they didn't film that.

Night in the House of Cards

A lot of dust has settled today,
The Evening News said.
The walls still shook from time to time
As if the night was a truck
Loaded with gravel rumbling by.

Then it was quiet.
The builder of the house of cards
Had rushed off
Holding her masked children by the hand.
I didn't dare light another match
And look at the walls.
There were pictures everywhere of bearded men
And their bearded wives.
The match flame made them dance
So that afterwards
I lay sleepless in the dark.

In the night, the wind
That chills the stars to a squint
Blew a card off the roof
Up one of its dark sleeves.
The dawn sky was like a torn red dress
The girl on the back of the card wore.

What the Gypsies Told My Grandmother while She Was Still a Young Girl

War, illness and famine will make you their favorite
    grandchild.
You'll be like a blind person watching a silent movie.
You'll chop onions and pieces of your heart into the same
    hot skillet.
Your children will sleep in a suitcase tied with a rope.
Your husband will kiss your breasts every night as if they
    were two gravestones.

Already the crows are grooming themselves for you and
    your people.
Your oldest son will lie with flies on his lips without smiling
    or lifting his hand.
You'll envy every ant you meet in your life and every
    roadside weed.
Your body and soul will sit on separate stoops chewing the
    same piece of gum.

Little cutie, are you for sale? the devil will say.
The undertaker will buy a toy for your grandson.
Your mind will be a hornet's nest even on your deathbed.
You will pray to God but God will hang a sign that He's not
    to be disturbed.
Question no further, that's all I know.

Have You Met Miss Jones?

I have. At the funeral
Pulling down her skirt to cover her knees
While inadvertently
Showing us her cleavage
Down to the tip of her nipples.

A complete stranger, wobbly on her heels,
Negotiating the exit
With the assembled mourners
Eyeing her rear end
With visible interest.

Presidential hopefuls
Will continue to lie to the people
As we sit here bowed.
New hatreds will sweep the globe
Faster than the weather.
Sewer rats will sniff around
Lit cash machines
While we sigh over the departed.

And her beauty will live on, no matter
What any one of these black-clad,
Grim veterans of every wake,
Every prison gate and crucifixion,
Sputters about her discourtesy.

Miss Jones, you'll be safe
With the insomniacs. You'll triumph
Where they pour wine from a bottle
Wrapped in a white napkin,
Eat sausage with pan-fried potatoes,
And grow misty-eyed remembering

The way you walked past the open coffin,
Past the stiff with his nose in the air
Taking his long siesta.
A cute little number an old man said,
But who was she?
Miss Jones, the guest book proclaimed.

On the Sagging Porch

Sits the grim-looking president
Of the local SPCA
As you come walking on all fours,
Making it plain you are lost,
Have a bad limp,
Need a brand-new master today.

He can use a stick if he wants to.
You desire an insignificant,
Silent and mostly sedentary life,
With your travels reduced
To one or two dark corners
And an occasional visit to the kitchen.

He makes no sign to acknowledge you.
His eyes are far away.
Is he blind, is he crazy?
You keep asking yourself.
His dog, coming over to sniff
And growl at you a little,
Is called Judas.

Dogs Hear It

This machinery is very ancient.
It lumbers towards me
With all its rusty parts throbbing.
A great big contraption made of air,
Made of phantasms.
Its wheels sulk. Dust chokes them,
Nasty bits of gravel
Full of their own spunk.

Some nights it's so loud,
I sit up in bed.
Hamlet's ghost walking the hallways
Of a motel in Vegas –

He draweth likeness after likeness
Of what's hidden in plain sight –
Who? Who? I shouted, startled,
Until the bride and groom next door
Told me to rest my jaws.

Ghosts

It's Mr Brown looking much better
Than he did in the morgue.
He's brought me a huge carp
In a bloodstained newspaper.
What an odd visit.
I haven't thought of him in years.

Linda is with him and so is Sue.
Two pale and elegant fading memories
Holding each other by the hand.
Even their lipstick is fresh
Despite all the scientific proofs
To the contrary.

Is Linda going to cook the fish?
She turns and gazes in the direction
Of the kitchen while Sue
Continues to watch me mournfully.
I don't believe any of it,
And still I'm scared stiff.

I know of no way to respond,
So I do nothing.
The windows are open. The air's thick
With the scent of magnolias.
Drops of evening rain are dripping
From the dark and heavy leaves.
I take a deep breath; I close my eyes.

Dear specters, I don't even believe
You are here, so how is it
You're making me comprehend
Things I would rather not know just yet?

It's the way you stare past me
At what must already be my own ghost,
Before taking your leave,
As unexpectedly as you came in,
Without one of us breaking the silence.

Theatrical Costumes

A present from neighborly burglars
For us to dress up
On a dull day
In a manner fantastic

Cutting a great dash
As we descend the stairs
In our powdered wigs and high-heeled shoes
Into the busy street,
Crossing it against the screeching
Traffic, and entering
The Burger Heaven with a swish
Of your long skirts
And not even a Say what?
From the astonished customers.

You are dressed like Marie Antoinette
And I am all in black
Like her executioner,
Or her father confessor.
It's New York City. It's hot.
The fire alarms are ringing everywhere.

The French Queen is putting
A lot of ketchup on her fries.
Her executioner is inserting
A lit ciggie in each ear
And blowing the smoke out his mouth.

At the Cookout

The wives of my friends
Have the air
Of having shared a secret.
Their eyes are lowered
But when we ask them
What for
They only glance at each other
And smile,
Which only increases our desire
To know . . .

Something they did
Long ago,
Heedless of the consequences,
That left
Such a lingering sweetness?

Is that the explanation
For the way
They rest their chins
In the palms of their hands,
Their eyes closed
In the summer heat?

Come tell us,
Or give us a hint.
Trace a word or just a single letter

In the wine
Spilled on the table.

No reply. Both of them
Lovey-dovey
With the waning sunlight
And the evening breeze
On their faces.

The husbands drinking
And saying nothing,
Dazed and mystified as they are
By their wives' power
To give
And take away happiness,
As if their heads
Were crawling with snakes.

Pastoral Harpsichord

A house with a screened-in porch
On the road to nowhere.
The missus topless because of the heat,
A bag of Frito Banditos in her lap.
President Bush on TV
Watching her every bite.

Poor reception, that's the one
Advantage we have here,
I said to the mutt lying at my feet
And sighing in sympathy.
On another channel the preacher
Came chaperoned by his ghost
When he shut his eyes full of tears
To pray for dollars.

'Bring me another beer,' I said to her ladyship,
And when she wouldn't oblige,
I went out to make chamber music
Against the sunflowers in the yard.

Entertaining the Canary

Yellow feathers,
Is it true
You chirp to the cop
On the beat?

Desist. Turn your
Nervous gaze
At the open bathroom door
Where I'm soaping

My love's back
And putting my chin on her shoulder
So I can do the same for her
Breasts and crotch.

Sing. Flutter your wings
As if you were applauding,
Or I'll throw her black slip
Over your gilded cage.

The Forest Walk

Today we took a long walk in the forest.
There we met a couple walking
Arm in arm with eyes closed.
The forest is a dream you had
When you were little, they told us.
Then the two of them were gone.

Even in the afternoon the narrow path
Was busy with shadows.
They had many dark secrets among them,
The trees did.
Shhhh is all we kept hearing.
The leaf we plucked and held in our hands
Appeared genuinely frightened.

The night threw open its birdcage.
The trees pretended to protect us.
In a fit of passion they'd rise
Against the slightest sough of wind,
Only to fall back
Into long minutes of listening.

Let's stay here tonight, you said,
And I agreed, but then we didn't.
You had left the key in the car,
And the video store was about to close.

We were running now.
We could see the ice-cream truck.
We could see the plane's landing lights.

Slaughterhouse Flies

Evenings, they ran their bloody feet
Over the pages of my schoolbooks.
With eyes closed, I can still hear
The trees on our street
Saying a moody farewell to summer,

And someone, under our window, recalling
The silly old cows hesitating,
Growing suddenly suspicious
Just as the blade drops down on them.

October Light

That same light by which I saw her last
Made me close my eyes now in revery,
Remembering how she sat in the garden

With a red shawl over her shoulders
And a small book in her lap,
Once in a long while looking up

With the day's brightness on her face,
As if to appraise something of utmost seriousness
She has just read at least twice,

With the sky clear and open to view,
Because the leaves had already fallen
And lay still around her two feet.

Sunset's Coloring Book

The blue trees argue with the red wind.

The white mare has a peacock for a servant.

The hawk brings the night in its claws.

The golden mountain doesn't exist.

The golden mountain touches the black sky.

In a Forest of Whispers

There is a blind hen
Pecking at a grain of gold
A stream so cold
It's afraid to flow

An escaped convict talking of home
To a withered tree
And death's favorite crow
Sitting in it

In a forest of whispers
Where a lone ant
Just raised on his back
A charred straw

Club Midnight

Are you the sole owner of a seedy nightclub?

Are you its sole customer, sole bartender,
Sole waiter prowling around the empty tables?

Do you put on wee-hour girlie shows
With dead stars of black-and-white films?

Is your office upstairs over the neon lights,
Or down deep in the dank rat cellar?

Are bearded Russian thinkers your silent partners?
Do you have a doorman by the name of Dostoyevsky?

Is Fu Manchu coming tonight?
Is Miss Emily Dickinson?

Do you happen to have an immortal soul?
Do you have a sneaky suspicion that you have none?

Is that why you throw a white pair of dice,
In the dark, long after the joint closes?

Late Call

A message for you,
Piece of shit:

You double-crossed us.
You were supposed to get yourself
Crucified
For the sake of Truth . . .

Who, me?

A mere crumb, thankfully,
Overlooked on a dinner table,
Lacking in enthusiasm . . .
An average nobody.

Oh, the worries . . .

In the dark windowpane
My mouth gutted open.
Aghast.
The panel of judges all black-hooded.

It must be a joke.
A misunderstanding, fellows.
A wrong number, surely?
A slipup?
An erratum?

The Street Ventriloquist

The bearded old man on the corner,
The one drinking out of a brown paper bag,
The one who declares himself
The world's greatest ventriloquist,
We are all his puppets, he says
When he chooses to say anything.

Neon at sundown, lovers carrying tall cages
With frightened songbirds,
Early shadows going to meet
The one and true darkness,
A few sun-struck windows at the horizon,
The blind doomsayer lifting his board
For all to read.

So, I'm the cat's-paw, I said,
And went off shadowboxing
With my own reflection
Appearing and disappearing
In a row of store windows
That already had that seen-a-ghost look.

Against Winter

The truth is dark under your eyelids.
What are you going to do about it?
The birds are silent; there's no one to ask.
All day long you'll squint at the gray sky.
When the wind blows you'll shiver like straw.

A meek little lamb, you grew your wool
Till they came after you with huge shears.
Flies hovered over your open mouth,
Then they, too, flew off like the leaves,
The bare branches reached after them in vain.

Winter coming. Like the last heroic soldier
Of a defeated army, you'll stay at your post,
Head bared to the first snowflake.
Till a neighbor comes to yell at you,
You're crazier than the weather, Charlie.

The Something

Here come my night thoughts
On crutches,
Returning from studying the heavens.
What they thought about
Stayed the same,
Stayed immense and incomprehensible.

My mother and father smile at each other
Knowingly above the mantel.
The cat sleeps on, the dog
Growls in his sleep.
The stove is cold and so is the bed.

Now there are only these crutches
To contend with.
Go ahead and laugh, while I raise one
With difficulty,
Swaying on the front porch,
While pointing at something
In the gray distance.

You see nothing, eh?
Neither do I, Mr Milkman.

I better hit you once or twice over the head
With this fine old prop,
So you don't go off muttering

I saw *something*.

The Emperor

Wears a pig mask
Over his face.

Sits in a shopping cart,

A red toy trumpet in one hand,
A live fly in the other.

Hey, boogie alley Madonna!

I'm donning my black cape
And my orange wraparound shades

Just for you!

*

The Garden of Eden needs weeding,

And the soda machines don't work.

On the street of Elvis look-alikes
I saw the Klan Wizard in his robes.

I saw the panhandling Jesus
And heard the sweet wind chime in his head.

*

It's horror movie time,
Says the Emperor.

Spiked hair, black flag of bug killers
In his belt,

He helps my frail old mother
Cross the street.

She's charmed and thanks him repeatedly:
'Such a nice boy,'

In the meantime,

Touching the mask's empty eye sockets
With her gloved hand.

*

On the graveyard shift,

Commands the Emperor,

Amplify the roaches crawling up
The kitchen wall.

Let's hear about their tuxes-for-rent places,

Their exotic dancers,

And their witch trials,

If they are the same as the ones we've got.

*

The child in a shoebox smoking
A black cigarillo.

The priest with a fly-catcher
At the altar.

The Emperor and the three-legged dog poet
By his side

Limping down the avenue.

*

Make us see what you see in your head,
We implore.

Okay.

He's climbing a ladder licked by flames.

He wears General Washington's wig and military coat.

He's inside a hamster cage admiring himself in the mirror.

He is playing with a million broken toys.